ASTRONAUT
TRAINING

ASTRONAUT TRAINING

**ANN ARMBRUSTER
AND
ELIZABETH A. TAYLOR**

FRANKLIN WATTS
NEW YORK/LONDON/TORONTO/SYDNEY
A FIRST BOOK ➤ 1990

All photographs courtesy of:
National Aeronautics and Space Administration.

Library of Congress Cataloging-in-Publication Data

Armbruster, Ann.
    Astronaut training / Ann Armbruster, Elizabeth A. Taylor.
        p.   c.m.—(A First book.)
    Summary: Describes the selection and training of astronauts.
    ISBN 0-531-10862-7
    1. Astronauts—Juvenile literature.   [1. Astronauts.]
  I. Taylor, Elizabeth A.   II. Title.   III. Series.
  TL793.A75   1990
  629.45'07—dc20   90-32894 CIP AC

CONTENTS

United States Senate

COMMITTEE ON
GOVERNMENTAL AFFAIRS

WASHINGTON, DC 20510–6250

JOHN GLENN, OHIO, CHAIRMAN

SAM NUNN, GEORGIA
CARL LEVIN, MICHIGAN
JIM SASSER, TENNESSEE
DAVID PRYOR, ARKANSAS
JEFF BINGAMAN, NEW MEXICO
HERBERT KOHL, WISCONSIN
JOSEPH I. LIEBERMAN, CONNECTICUT

WILLIAM V. ROTH, JR., DELAWARE
TED STEVENS, ALASKA
WILLIAM S. COHEN, MAINE
WARREN B. RUDMAN, NEW HAMPSHIRE
JOHN HEINZ, PENNSYLVANIA
PETE WILSON, CALIFORNIA

LEONARD WEISS, STAFF DIRECTOR
JO ANNE BARNHART, MINORITY STAFF DIRECTOR

Dear Girls and Boys:

In 1962 I became the first American to orbit the Earth and look down on our planet from space. From my orbit over 100 miles high the Earth looked blue-green beneath lacy white clouds and I was filled with a sense of wonder I will never forget.

I know that many of you are just as excited as I have been about space and its possibilities. We are only getting started at space exploration, and there are wonderful discoveries out there, waiting for you and your generation to make them. Some of you may choose to make space a lifelong study or career. But whatever your aspirations, I hope each of you will study hard, mastering the basic skills of learning -- curiosity and questioning, research and reporting, and critical thinking and debating -- so that our future explorations of our universe will expand our scientific knowledge and benefit all of humanity.

I also hope that while you are learning you will always try to be friendly and fair with one another, and practice the democracy that is so important for freedom, security and peace among all the people of our beautiful planet home.

Best regards.

Sincerely,

John Glenn

John Glenn
United States Senator

JG/ca

Letter from John Glenn

WHAT IS AN ASTRONAUT?

Have you ever stood outside on a clear, cool evening and looked up at the stars and the endless space surrounding them? Perhaps you have imagined yourself as an astronaut (a man or woman who pilots a spacecraft) exploring other planets and taking a trip to other worlds.

Astronauts are space travelers, but they don't fly around the universe as easily as Superman. To get a proper look at astronauts, turn the lens of your imaginary telescope on these men and women. You will see that they have

➤ excellent physical health
➤ ability to perform under stress
➤ willingness to spend long hours in training
➤ a desire to explore
➤ adaptability to living in space

Now turn the lens of this same telescope on yourself. Examine your ambitions, attitudes, and dreams about the future. If you possess some of these same traits, you might consider becoming an astronaut—an explorer of the space frontier.

THE EARLY ASTRONAUTS

2

Space is that part of the universe lying outside the limits of Earth's atmosphere. Near Earth's surface, air is plentiful. High above Earth, the air becomes thinner, and gradually the atmosphere disappears.

Sending a person into this void known as space is much more complicated than sending mechanical instruments. People are well adapted to living in the Earth's atmosphere where air is plentiful, food is available, and gravity controls our upright position. Space is a dark, hostile environment with extreme temperatures, meteors, and radiation. Space travelers have experienced intense feelings of isolation and loneliness.

The space race began in October 1957, when the Russians launched the first artificial satellite, *Sputnik I*. In November 1957 they launched *Sputnik II* with a dog, Laika, aboard. This flight proved that living creatures could survive in space. The Russians achieved another

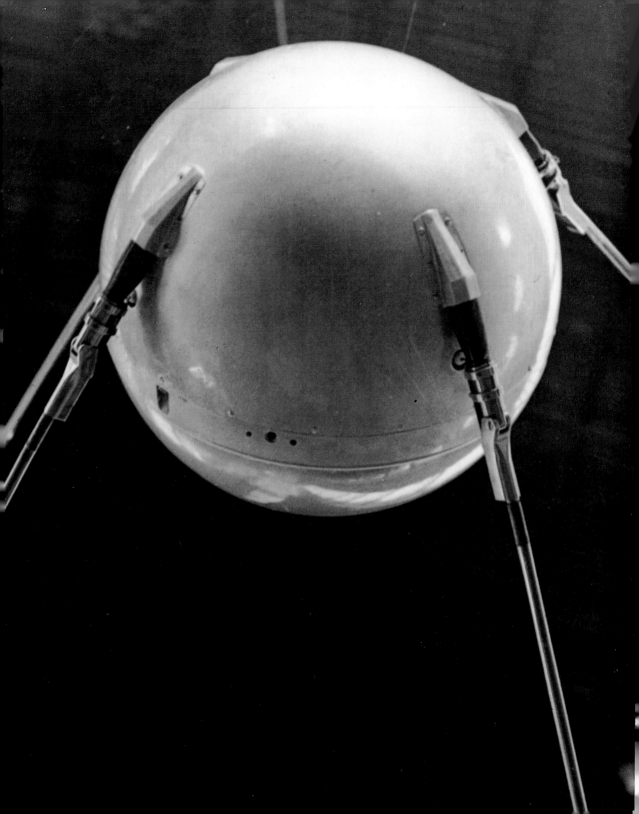

record in 1961, when Yuri Gagarin, the world's first cosmonaut (a Soviet astronaut), circled Earth for 108 minutes in his spacecraft *Vostok I*.

In order to regain leadership in the scientific community, and to compete with the Russians, the United States organized the National Aeronautics and Space Administration (NASA) in 1958. This organization was to direct the country's space program.

PROJECT MERCURY

The first American manned spaceflight was Project Mercury, named for the famous winged messenger of the gods. The objectives of this project were to orbit a manned spacecraft around Earth, obtain information about human capabilities in space, and bring that knowledge back to Earth.

In 1959 NASA chose the country's 7 original astronauts from 508 applicants. They were Gordon Cooper, Walter Schirra, Alan Shepard, John Glenn, Scott Car-

A full-scale mock-up of the Russian Sputnik I *spacecraft—the first real voyager into space.*

penter, Donald Slayton, and Virgil Grissom. These seven were all men, all military test pilots, all in their 30s, and all married. Only steady, mature applicants were considered eligible to be the first explorers in space. One of the primary requirements was the ability not to panic under stress. Lives could depend on one person's reaction to problems while traveling through space at 17,900 miles per hour.

Astronauts have to be in excellent physical shape to survive the rigorous training that is required. None of the original Project Mercury astronauts could be taller than 5 feet 11 inches (177.5 cm) because of the small size of the space capsule. They were X-rayed, their brain waves were measured, and their eyes were examined. Hearts, circulatory systems, stomach muscles, bones, and glands were all checked with the greatest care.

To test their ability to function in high temperatures, the astronauts were subjected to temperatures of 150°F (65°C) for two hours and alternately immersed in ice baths to check their reaction to cold. They were sometimes kept in soundproof rooms while doctors checked readings for pulse, blood pressure, and respiration.

When the astronauts were fitted for space suits, their bodies were dotted with ink spots and then photographed. By studying their body contours, technicians were able to fit each astronaut with a space suit and design the contour couch for their space capsule.

The seven-member first astronaut team
included: (front row from left to right)
Walter Schirra, Donald Slayton, John Glenn,
Scott Carpenter, and (back row) Alan Shepard,
Virgil Grissom, and Gordon Cooper.

The space suit designed for Project Mercury was modeled after the first U.S. Navy Mark IV pressure suit used in high-speed flight. It was a four-layered suit with a padded helmet to prevent head injury. Oxygen was fed into the suit through a connector located in the torso area; custom-made boots and gloves were also part of the outfit.

During Project Mercury, a good portion of the astronauts' time was spent in the classroom studying the basic sciences. By the time the first space capsule was launched, each astronaut had enough classroom time to qualify for a master's degree in the sciences. All the original trainees were also required to have at least 1,500 hours of flying time.

The original seven astronauts ate cubed foods and puréed meats, vegetables, and fruits that were packaged in flexible aluminum tubes. This type of food has many advantages because it weighs only one tenth as much as ordinary food and can be stored in plastic bags at room temperature without spoiling.

Vomit Comet ➢ One of the primary concerns of Project Mercury was how astronauts could handle the problems of weightlessness (a condition of almost no gravity) while wearing heavy space suits and carrying awkward life-support systems on their backs.

Astronaut Donald Slayton sits for a space suit fitting.

Left: John Glenn performs a respiratory test as part of the NASA flight training program.

Right: astronaut candidates today undergo zero-gravity training in a KC-135 aircraft, as did Project Mercury astronauts.

To train for this experience, astronauts were taken for rides in the KC-135 jet aircraft, nicknamed the Vomit Comet. The astronauts experienced weightlessness for 20 to 22 seconds as the aircraft climbed and dived. Nausea was often a side effect of this exercise.

Completion of Project ➤ In 1961 Alan Shepard proved the success of this project when he made a suborbital flight of Earth in the spacecraft *Freedom 7.* He reached a height of 116.5 miles (186 km), with the entire trip lasting only about 15 minutes.

Another Project Mercury success was achieved on February 20, 1962, when John Glenn, in his spacecraft *Friendship 7,* became the first person to orbit Earth. He was in space for 4 hours, 55 minutes, 23 seconds. A record had been set, and the way had been paved for future projects in which space travelers would spend long periods of time in space.

PROJECT GEMINI

In the mid-1960s, the second U.S. manned spaceflight project, Gemini, was started. It was named for the constellation Gemini, or the Twins—Castor and Pollux. NASA adopted this name for the two-person space program aimed at sending "space twins" into orbit around Earth.

The objectives of this project were to collect data on the performance of astronauts during prolonged flights and to practice the techniques used in the rendezvous and docking of two spacecraft. This knowledge would be important for a future lunar (Moon) landing.

Classroom courses for the Gemini program were broader in scope than those for Project Mercury. Flight

Above: weightlessness and other training prepared John Glenn for the experience of traveling 17,500 mph in Friendship 7. *Right: astronauts James McDivitt and Edward White train for the* Gemini 4 *mission in a simulated launch.*

mechanics, space communications, and survival techniques were added to the basic science curriculum to prepare astronauts for longer periods of survival in space.

Eating on the Gemini mission was easier than it had been for the Mercury astronauts. Food chunks were coated with an edible gelatin to reduce crumbling, and freeze-dried food was rehydrated (fluid replaced) by the use of a water gun.

A Walk in Space ➢ The most dramatic mission of the Gemini project took place on June 3, 1965, when Astronaut Edward White took a 23-minute walk. Astronaut White carried a compressed gas unit, nicknamed "the gun," that he could use to propel himself in any direction. While outside the spacecraft, he was connected by a 24-foot (7-m) communications line that the media called "an umbilical cord" (the cord that attaches a fetus to the mother).

To prepare for this first "walk in space," Astronaut Edward White's training included using the Hand-held Self-maneuvering Unit and the emergency oxygen supply chest pack.

Completion of Project ➤ Project Gemini proved that astronauts could survive for longer periods in space and could also function effectively outside the spacecraft. The astronauts also completed the first successful space rendezvous and docking of two spacecraft when *Gemini 6* and *Gemini 7* were maneuvered within 120 feet (36 m) of each other.

PROJECT APOLLO

With the successful completion of Projects Mercury and Gemini, the United States was ready to attempt the third stage of the Moon exploration program: to land an astronaut on the Moon. The earlier projects had shown that weightlessness is tolerable for extended periods of time and that humans can function outside the environment of a spacecraft.

The massive Apollo effort was aimed at landing an astronaut on the Moon, completing a program of scientific discovery of the Moon, and developing skills necessary to work in a lunar environment. The sum of $23 billion was needed to complete this mission, in addition to 20,000 companies and 400,000 workers.

During the *Apollo 11* flight, picking up soil samples with a long-handled scoop was the astronauts' priority assignment. Special tools were developed for space repair and construction. A tether (the ''umbilical cord'') enabled them to leave the orbiting space vehicle and

Apollo astronauts Neil Armstrong (in background) and Edwin Aldrin study rock samples during a geological field trip in Texas to prepare for collecting Moon rocks.

complete the scientific experiments with more ease. Because of space travelers' weightlessness, they are unable to exert the same forces that are possible within the earth's gravity.

➤ 23

Apollo astronaut Edwin Aldrin trained in an Extravehicular Mobility Unit on a simulated Moon surface.

*Apollo astronauts trained to work outside
the spacecraft; Harrison Schmitt here
collects samples with a lunar scoop.*

The space suit for the Apollo project had 21 pressurized layers. Water tubes were threaded through the wearer's underwear for cooling against the blazing sun, and a backpack stored water, oxygen, and control equipment. The suit weighed 180 pounds (81 kg), took 45 minutes to get into, and cost $300,000 per suit. It protected the astronauts from extreme temperatures of -250 to $+250°F$ (-121 to $+121°C$) (the extreme temperatures of a lunar day).

Astronaut on the Moon ➤ On July 16, 1969, a giant Saturn V rocket sent three astronauts (Neil Armstrong, Edwin Aldrin, and Michael Collins) to the Moon in the spacecraft *The Eagle*. They landed on Tranquility Base on July 20, 1969.

Project Apollo achieved the agelong dream of landing a person on the Moon. It also paved the way for future space exploration and discovery. Neil Armstrong left two American symbols behind: an American flag and a plaque bearing the words ''We came in peace for all mankind.''

WHO HAS THE RIGHT STUFF?

3

In 1987, 1,962 people applied to NASA to become astronauts; only 15 were chosen. These were representative of America's best-qualified scientists, engineers, and pilots.

Until 1985 NASA issued a call whenever it was decided that a new class of astronauts was needed. Notices were sent to colleges and universities and to newspapers and television and radio stations. Today NASA encourages people who are interested in becoming astronauts to apply at any time.

NASA officials emphasize that they look for a strong educational background when applicants are considered for selection. All astronauts must have at least a bachelor's degree in engineering, biological or physical sciences, or mathematics from an accredited (meeting certain standards) college or university.

TYPES OF ASTRONAUTS

Some applicants want to be pilot astronauts. Pilot astronauts specialize in flying the shuttle and make up the command crew (shuttle pilot and shuttle commander). Pilot candidates must have at least 1,000 hours' experience as a pilot in command of a high-performance jet aircraft. It helps if the person has worked as a test pilot. The pilot candidate must be able to pass a NASA class I spaceflight physical and be between 64 and 76 inches (160–190 cm) in height.

Space Shuttle commander Donald Williams and the pilot (with his back to the camera) appear at their work stations.

*Mission Specialist Guion Bluford
checks an on-board experiment.*

Some applicants want to be mission specialist (MS) astronauts. Mission specialists work with the shuttle commander and pilot, and manage the activities aboard the shuttle. Mission specialist applicants must have a bachelor's degree and at least three years of related work experience. An advanced degree could be substituted for the experience (a master's degree = 1 year; a PhD degree = 3 years). MS applicants must pass a NASA class II space flight physical. The vision and hearing requirements are less strict than for the pilot applicants, but blood pressure standards are the same. Applicants must be between 60 and 76 inches (150–190 cm) tall.

A third type of astronaut is the payload specialist (PS) astronaut. Payload specialists are usually professional scientists who are not employed by NASA. They are selected by a customer who pays for their ride into space, where they perform experiments or do research for the customer company. They need not be U.S. citizens. All PS astronauts must meet NASA health and physical fitness standards. Payload specialists must have the education and training necessary for the payload experiment.

A fourth type of astronaut, the spaceflight participant, has recently been included in shuttle missions. Christa McAuliffe, the first spaceflight participant, was

Barbara Morgan, the teacher in space, and two other prospective spaceflight participants train in the KC-135 aircraft.

chosen as the Teacher-in-Space. After her death in the 1986 *Challenger* disaster, Barbara Morgan was named to that position. NASA hopes that a Journalist-in-Space program will follow.

CHOOSING THE ASTRONAUTS

When NASA is ready for a new class of astronauts, the applications on file are studied to determine which applicants are best qualified.

In the next step in the selection process, those applicants who are best qualified are brought to Houston's Johnson Space Center for interviews and testing. Most astronauts say they had no idea what to expect during the weeklong series of tests and were more than a little worried about how they would perform.

Because all astronauts must be in top physical condition, fitness tests are done first. Applicants must also take hearing and speech tests. Flight doctors are not looking for superhumans, but everyone on a mission must be healthy and strong enough to do his or her share.

Not every physically fit applicant is suited to become an astronaut. Applicants must undergo psychological testing as well, to predict how they might react under pressure, how they feel about performing as team members, and how well they might be able to give or follow directions. Every part of the applicants' personalities must be studied to decide how well they might

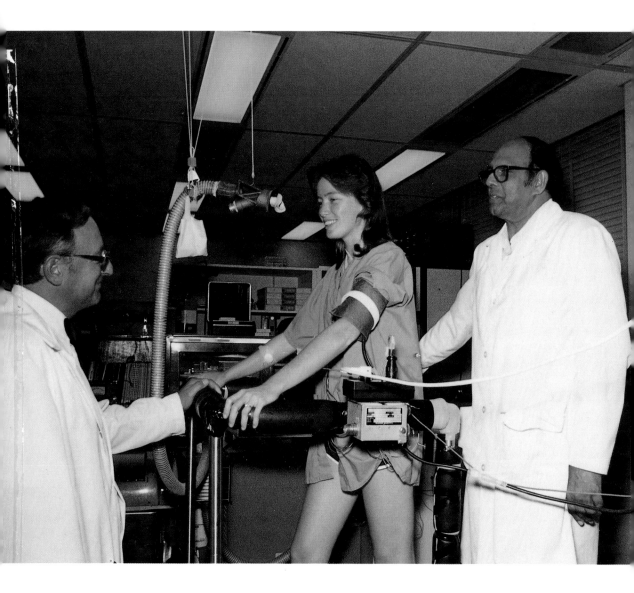

Astronaut applicant Dr. Anna Fisher prepares for a treadmill test at the Johnson Space Center cardiopulmonary laboratories.

perform under the stressful conditions of a shuttle mission. A quick reaction could save the lives of crew members during an emergency.

Psychiatrists must also weed out applicants who have claustrophobia (fear of being enclosed in small spaces). Although today's shuttles are luxurious compared to the Mercury, Gemini, and Apollo capsules, they are still small spaces.

Persistence is a trait NASA values in its astronauts. Some astronauts were chosen after applying as many as five times. Having been turned down, they went home to sharpen their skills, gain more experience, and add to their educational background. Then they went back for another try.

The final test an astronaut must pass is an interview with the astronaut selection committee. Most of the committee members are active astronauts who know what they would like to see in another astronaut or crew mate. They are not looking for superstars, but are interested in finding flexible people who can adapt to new and dangerous situations.

After the weeklong testing and interview at Johnson Center, the selection committee interviews the applicants' co-workers and family members and conducts security checks to help them make a final decision. Once the selections are made, the candidates enter the first phase of astronaut training, during which they are called astronaut candidates, or "ascans."

4 TRAINING TODAY'S ASTRONAUTS

Most astronauts have said that becoming an astronaut candidate (ascan) was a dream come true, even though the training schedule may seem more like a nightmare. Their studies include learning everything there is to know about shuttle construction, preparing for medical and mechanical emergencies aboard the shuttle, and mastering the tricks of daily living in space.

BASIC TRAINING

During their year of *basic training,* ascans attend lectures and use workbooks and computers just as you do. Pilot astronaut candidates take flight training. Much basic training is done on the job, and ascans are expected to help in the development of shuttle equipment.

When ascans graduate from basic training, they become members of the astronaut corps. Now they are called astronauts and enter the training pool. In the training pool

Training for the ascans includes parachute-drop simulations.

they work at keeping their skills sharp while they wait to be called to fly a mission.

ADVANCED TRAINING

Once a mission has been assigned, those astronauts chosen are given *advanced* and *flight-specific* training. Advanced training lets astronauts practice using every system in the shuttle. Using computerized models of parts of the shuttle, astronauts practice flying and landing the shuttle, operating the remote-controlled arm, and even using the sewage and waste removal system. The most important model is the Shuttle Mission Simulator (SMS). This computer can take the crew from 30 minutes before launch to landing and rollout (after the wheels stop).

On board the Space Shuttle Mission Simulator, the crew take their launch positions for the next spaceflight.

FLIGHT-SPECIFIC TRAINING

Flight-specific training is practice for one specific flight. During each mission the crew has a list of jobs that must be done perfectly. This training begins eleven weeks before the mission takes place. The mission plan is loaded into the SMS. From then on, crew members work as a team, rehearsing every part of the flight. At the same time, the mission control team follows the crew's progress at their SMS computer stations.

It usually takes five years for an astronaut to be trained and assigned a mission. When the mission is completed, the astronaut returns to the training pool to await another flight. There basic and advanced skills are practiced every day.

MOVING AROUND IN SPACE

Many simple tasks become difficult in space and take practice to perform. Crossing a room must be done very

Astronauts Michael McCulley and Ellen Baker experience their first meal in a zero-gravity environment.

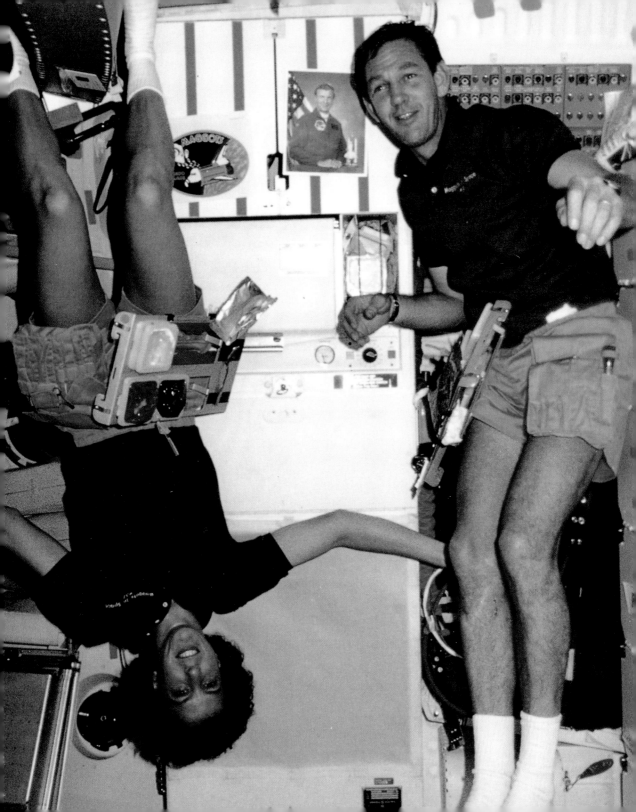

carefully in zero gravity (a condition in which a body follows the pull of gravity freely without resisting the pull in any way). *Zero gravity* is a term astronauts use, but the public usually uses the term *weightlessness.*

Astronauts do not walk. They float or glide from place to place inside the shuttle. Floating sounds easy, but it can be difficult, frustrating, and dangerous. Ascans practice moving about in orbit by riding in a KC-135 aircraft just as the early astronauts did.

WORKING OUTSIDE
THE SHUTTLE

The shuttle's interior is a short-sleeves environment. The pressure, temperature, and humidity are controlled so that the astronauts can wear lightweight, flexible clothing. Flexible clothing is important because of the cramped conditions and the need to use arms as well as legs to go from one part of the shuttle to another. However, not all of the astronauts' work is done inside the shuttle.

Bruce McCandless was the first astronaut to use the bulky MMU (Manned Mobility Unit) to work outside the shuttle. The MMU is quite heavy on earth but not in space. Its wearer controls tiny jets of air that push the astronaut in the desired direction. How can astronauts learn to use the MMU before going into space? They practice in a pool at the Wet-F (Weightless Environment

Facility) at the Johnson Space Center and at the NBS (Neutral Buoyancy Simulator). The NBS is a water-filled tank 150 feet (47 m) deep and 75 feet (24 m) wide, with a capacity of 1.3 million gallons, at the Marshall Space Center in Huntsville, Alabama. A scuba diver who is properly weighted neither sinks nor rises to the tank's surface. Before using the Wet-F or the NBS, ascans must pass a scuba diving course.

The Weightless Environment Training Facility (Wet-F) is used for crew instruction in a simulated space environment.

Astronauts say that being in the NBS feels much like being in space. Of course, the training must be as realistic as possible, so the heavy EMU (Extravehicular Mobility Unit) suit must be worn. The suits are made of pieces that are selected to fit the individual astronaut. Because the suits are so expensive, not many can be made. That is one reason astronauts must fit within height and weight limits.

Once the astronaut is suited up, he or she enters the NBS, where work is provided using a mock-up of the shuttle bay compartment in the tank. The astronaut must first find a handhold or foothold to provide an anchor while working. Otherwise the astronaut would float away from the job, just as in space. Astronauts usually spend several months training in the large NBS in Huntsville or the smaller Wet-F in Houston.

Astronaut John Fabian, wearing a pressurized Extravehicular Mobility Unit (EMU) prepares to go underwater in the Wet-F.

*Shuttle astronauts Sally Ride and
Frederick Hauck check procedures to
operate the Remote Manipulator System
(RMS) in an engineering simulator.*

Working in space is difficult too because heavy gloves must be worn to protect the hands. The gloves have flexible rubber finger caps, but working in them is a little like threading a needle while your hands are asleep.

A giant 50-foot (16-m)-long robot arm, the Remote Manipulator System (RMS) is folded and carried in the shuttle's cargo bay. It can reach out to pick a satellite out of orbit with ease if a skilled operator controls it. On Earth, ascans practice using the robot arm until they can retrieve satellites during every attempt. One of the most skilled RMS operators, scientist-astronaut Sally Ride studied the RMS during its development and testing on Earth and helped in mission control when it was space-tested in November 1987.

EXPERIMENTS AND TESTS

The shuttle was designed to be a space laboratory as well as a space truck. Experiments conducted in space are designed by people who want to know the effects of zero gravity on plants, animals, people, and nonliving substances. Corporations, universities, and the federal government pay for these tests and experiments to be done aboard the shuttle. Scientists-astronauts practice doing the experiments many times before taking them into orbit. Of course, the results will be different in space, but the procedures are the same.

A mission specialist and two Spacelab payload specialists at work in the Spacelab 1 module aboard the Earth-orbiting Space Shuttle Columbia.

EVERYDAY ACTIVITIES

Learning to maneuver in space is basic to all other types of astronaut training because no activity can be done the same way in space as it is on Earth. Even eating takes practice. Before you eat, you usually sit down. Not in space. Sitting in a chair is difficult with so little gravity to hold you there. The strain on their stomach muscles, tensed to hold their legs in a sitting position, has convinced astronauts that floating around the shuttle middeck while eating is more comfortable and more sensible.

Before you eat, you wash your hands. So do astronauts, but in a very different way. The hand-washing unit is enclosed so that water drops won't escape and float around the cabin. Astronauts push their hands through openings in the chamber until flexible cuffs surround their wrists. A stream of water sprays the hands and is then sucked back into the disposal tank. Towel baths are taken using chemically treated washcloths.

The WCS (Waste Collection System), or toilet, looks like those on Earth except that a spring-mounted thigh bar is used to keep the astronauts seated. Sliding their toes into straps on the floor also helps astronauts stay in place.

Astronauts even have to learn to sleep in space. They cannot lie down to sleep because they would just float away. Instead of a bed, an astronaut can slumber in a

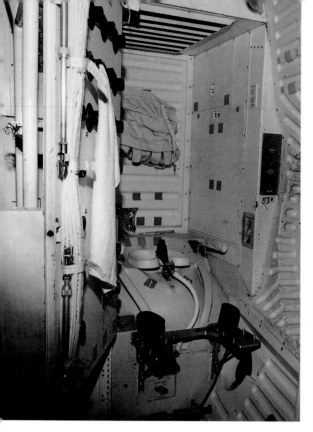

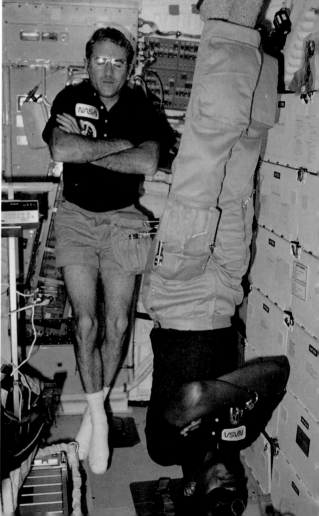

The Space Shuttle waste-collection system.

Commander Richard Truly and Mission Specialist Guion Bluford sleep at zero-gravity.

sleep restraint, a stiff pad with a sleeping bag attached. The bag is slightly inflated to make it feel like a mattress. Straps slipped over the arms keep them inside the bag.

MOCK-UPS AND SIMULATORS

How can astronauts prepare themselves for eating, sleeping, bathing, and using the bathroom in space? Ascans practice these activities in mock-ups of the shuttle middeck. Mock-ups are full-size models of all or part of the shuttle. In a mock-up every piece of equipment carried on the shuttle is in its customary place. A working model of a piece of equipment or a section of the shuttle is called a simulator. Simulators show astronauts how the shuttle is supposed to work. The simulators also provide practice in using equipment that isn't working properly. Astronauts must be prepared to repair or substitute equipment quickly in an emergency.

It costs an enormous amount of money every hour for every astronaut in orbit, so the astronauts must have practiced every job before the shuttle launch. While in training, ascans and members of the astronaut corps practice regularly in shuttle simulators. Before a mission, the training is increased to many sessions each week, with each session lasting eight to ten hours. Ninety-five

*Actual parachute jumps
are an important part
of ascan preparation.*

percent of the time in the simulators is spent practicing a situation gone wrong.

Even astronauts who are not jet pilots must have training in a flight deck simulator to learn to fly or land the shuttle during an emergency. They also train in a T-38 airplane. The T-38 is a two-seat trainer with dual controls. Ascans who have flight experience still must use the trainer and must fly often to keep in practice. Ascans learn and practice parachuting and ejecting from a T-38 in case something goes wrong with the aircraft and as an exercise in escaping from a disabled shuttle.

SHUTTLE ESCAPE

In November 1988, the shuttle flew again for the first time since January 28, 1986, when the *Challenger* space

The 36-inch-diameter fabric ball—the personal rescue sphere or system—is used to familiarize trainees with spending time in a small enclosed environment.

shuttle tragically exploded one minute after lift-off. The shuttle *Discovery,* piloted by Richard Covey and commanded by Rick Hauk, carried only seasoned members of the astronaut corps. They had trained intensively on simulators overhauled and redesigned to match the changes in *Discovery.* On launch day the whole world anxiously watched.

As the crew practiced, they were tested with a series of mock accidents in their simulators. To train for an

Astronauts and ground crews
participate in a simulated emergency
escape exercise on the launchpad.

Astronaut Neil Armstrong in a Gemini-type pressure suit after a simulated water landing.

escape, astronauts must know everything that could go wrong with the shuttle. Then they work with shuttle designers and other scientists to plan ways of escaping the shuttle while it is still on the launchpad, on the way toward orbit, and in orbit. The success of any escape depends on the crew's practicing until every move is automatic.

If astronauts parachute into the sea, the wilderness, or a desert, they will use their survival training to keep themselves and each other alive until help arrives. The training includes the use of emergency equipment, finding food and water, and first aid. To train, astronauts are taken into deep woods or dropped from helicopters into the sea—they are put into situations where their knowledge of first aid may save lives.

BODY CHANGES

Astronauts must learn to expect and deal with body changes in space. Because their bones do not bear weight, they lose calcium. Because muscles do not pull against the force of gravity, they become weak. Astronauts who spend weeks or months in orbit must learn to exercise on machines to prevent loss of muscle strength.

In orbit body fluids tend to move upward above the astronaut's waist. During reentry, special tight-fitting leggings must be worn so that body fluid does not drop quickly in response to gravity. If too much fluid (blood) suddenly leaves the brain, the astronaut would black out.

Astronauts suffer nasal congestion when fluid moves upward into the sinuses. Decongestants are always carried aboard shuttles.

In space, astronauts usually "grow" 1 to 2 inches (2.5–5 cm) in height because the disks between the vertebrae in the spine are no longer pulled together by gravity. Once back on Earth, they return to their usual height.

Nausea or space sickness is common. Most astronauts wear patches soaked in medicine behind an ear to help control nausea. It is also helpful if astronauts remember not to turn their heads quickly.

MENTAL TRAINING

Fear and anxiety must be controlled so that astronauts may do their jobs. Intense training helps astronauts gain confidence that they will react properly in an emergency.

Astronauts train to sharpen their skills in communicating with the public because they are often interviewed for news broadcasts and newspaper stories. They must be able to speak positively about their jobs and the space program.

SO YOU WANT TO BE AN ASTRONAUT

ASTRONAUT APPEAL

When you read about the public enthusiasm about the astronauts—Sally Ride, the first American woman to orbit the earth; Neil Armstrong, the first person to walk on the Moon; and others—it is easy to assume that an astronaut's life is one of constant excitement.

It is true that astronauts receive national attention, but don't let those brief moments of acclaim mislead you. Did you ever wonder how many years of education and training it requires to become an astronaut? If you are seriously interested in this work, start now to investigate the requirements and also the rewards of a most demanding profession.

ASTRONAUT FACT SHEET

An astronaut must have a bachelor's degree from an accredited college.

Astronauts study mathematics, meteorology, astronomy, physics, computers, biological sciences, and geology.

Astronauts must have at least 3 years of related professional experience.

Pilot astronauts must have at least 1,000 hours of training in a jet aircraft.

Astronauts must have excellent health.

Astronauts must learn to work as part of a team and also as individuals.

Astronauts must not panic under stress and must be adaptable.

LIFT-OFF

The frontiers of space are continually moving outward, and by the mid-1990s U.S. space travelers may be living and working in space. To fill the positions of mission specialists, payload specialists, and pilot astronauts, young men and women will have to possess special qualities.

So keep yourself physically fit with good eating habits and regular exercise. Keep yourself psychologically fit by developing good mental attitudes. Keep yourself educationally fit by exploring new ideas and sharpening your skills.

APPENDIX

RELATED ACTIVITIES

Today many students are interested in the space program. This was evident when 71,650 of them entered the ''Name the Orbiter'' contest sponsored by NASA. The name ''Endeavor'' was chosen for the space shuttle orbiter scheduled for completion in 1991.

In 1984 President Ronald Reagan initiated the Young Astronaut Program to stimulate the spirit of scientific inquiry in the nation's young people. Young Astronaut Clubs were formed in schools and communities around the country for students in three grade levels: 1 to 3, 4 to 6, and 7 to 9. Curriculum information and activities are designed specifically for each grade level.

The Boy Scouts of America now offer a merit badge in space exploration. Some of the ways you can earn this badge are to build, launch, and recover a model rocket. You can make a second launch to accomplish a specific mission objective. (The rocket must be built to meet the Safety Code of the National Association of Rocketry.) You could also tell the purposes of space exploration, including historical reason, immediate goals, benefits of "spin-offs," and values as related to earth resources.

Students aged 8 to 14 are eligible to join the Space Club. For an annual fee of $20 they receive comprehensive workbooks with lively illustrations and puzzles about the space program. A newsletter, *Space Camp News,* keeps them up to date on space history, space terminology, mission objectives, and space shuttle experiments.

If you are interested, write to U.S. Space Club, P.O. Box 1680, Huntsville, AL 35807.

High school students interested in the space program should follow a pre-college curriculum with emphasis on math and the sciences. In addition, they can write to various organizations concerned with space flight (some are listed in Information Sources later in this book) and talk with people employed as pilots or engineers in the space program.

The University of North Dakota now offers a minor program as well as a master's degree in space careers. Courses such as Introduction to Space Studies, Advanced Mission Design, and Life Support Systems are part of the program.

PLACES TO VISIT

National Air and Space Museum
Sixth Street and
Independence Avenue
Washington, DC 20560

Visiting hours: 10 A.M.–5:30 P.M. daily

Phone: (202) 357-1300

You will get a firsthand look at space history here. You can see some of the original space capsules used by the astronauts. Astronaut clothing is also on display. You can purchase freeze-dried food prepared by the same process they use in space. The lunar rover (the small vehicle used to explore the Moon's surface) and other space memorabilia are on display.

Johnson Space Center
Houston, TX 77058

Visiting hours: 9 A.M.–4 P.M. daily
Phone: (713) 483-3111

This center has been the setting for some history-making events. The first flight to the Moon was directed from here, and American astronauts are also trained here. You can write or call for information about tours and facilities.

Kennedy Space Center
Kennedy Space Center, FL 32891

Phone: (407) 867-7110

Kennedy Space Center, America's most famous "space port," is located on Merritt Island, Cape Canaveral, Florida. The center is the home of the shuttle launch pad. The visiting hours here are changeable, so write or call about specific times.

INFORMATION SOURCES

Aerospace Education Foundation
1750 Pennsylvania Avenue, NW
Washington, DC 20001

Aerospace Youth Council
1785 Massachusetts Avenue, NW
Washington, DC 20036

American Institute of Aeronautics and Astronautics
370 L'Enfant Promenade, SW
Washington, D.C. 20024-2518

Astronaut Candidate Program
Astronaut Selection Office, Mail Code AHX
Johnson Space Center
Houston, TX 77058

NASA, Educational Affairs Division
Office of External Relations
400 Maryland Avenue
Washington, DC 20025

National Aerospace Education Association
Shoreham Building, 806 15th Street, NW
Washington, DC 20005

U.S. Space Camp
The Space and Rocket Center
Tranquility Base
Huntsville, AL 35807

Young Astronaut Council
PO Box 65432
Washington, DC 20036

READING LIST

Clarke, A. C. *Man and Space*. New York: Time-Life Books, 1969.

Fox, Mary V. *Women Astronauts*. New York: Messner, 1984.

Gurney, Gene. *Americans into Orbit*. New York: Random House, 1962.

Hill, Robert W. *What the Moon Astronauts Do*. New York: John Day, 1963.

Human Spaceflight. Aerospace Education Services Project, NASA, Lewis Research Center, Cleveland, OH, 1985.

Merit Badge Requirements. North Brunswick, NJ: Boy Scouts of America, 1982.

MOD Training Division Overview. Houston: NASA, 1988.

O'Connor, Karen. *Sally Ride and the New Astronauts*. New York: Franklin Watts, 1983.

Schulke, Flip and Debra, McPhee, Penelope and Raymond. *Your Future in Space. The U.S. Space Camp® Training Program*, New York: Crown Publishers, 1986.

INDEX